Due

FRIENDS OF

Footprints

1951

FRIENDS OF

Footprints

*How **Footprints** has left its imprint on readers around the world*

MARGARET FISHBACK POWERS

HarperCollins*PublishersLtd*

First edition

Canadian Cataloguing in Publication Data

Powers, Margaret Fishback
Friends of Footprints : how Footprints has left its imprint
on readers around the world

ISBN 0-00-638520-6

1. Powers, Margaret Fishback - Correspondence.
2. Powers, Margaret Fishback. Footprints. I. Title.

PS8581.O94Z54 1996   C811′.54   C95-933314-2
PR9199.3.P68Z48 1996

96 97 98 99 ❖ EB 10 9 8 7 6 5 4 3 2 1

Printed and bound in the United States

The Author of Footprints
by the Reverend John T. Ballard

As Paul and Margaret went for a stroll along a beach near Kingston, Ontario, Paul tried to persuade Margaret to accept his marriage proposal. Looking back at their footprints, Paul ardently declared, "See our two sets of footprints in the sand? On our wedding day the two of us will become one. Oh, the joy that I will feel to carry you into eternity with the Lord." Margaret was not as ecstatic as Paul, and remembering her recent break-up countered his proposal with, "What happens when troubles come that we just can't handle?" Paul reassured her, "That's when the Lord will carry us both." Those words rang in Margaret's mind. Could they really be true, or would Paul demand more of her than she could produce? Everything was moving so fast that her mind felt like it would burst.

That night it was impossible to sleep. Every time Margaret closed her eyes she could see the footprints in the sand and she kept reflecting on this whirlwind of the day walking on the beach. Inspired to take pen and paper, Margaret began to write. She found her hand moving dream-like over the page. From deep inside flashed scenes from her past, and as each scene surfaced she sensed the Lord touching and healing her. She knew then that the Lord had been carrying her, even in her most troublesome times. He could be trusted to carry her through all of life's journey. She knew that God is love, and in that knowledge she could love again. That was the answer she needed and the answer she would give to Paul.

Looking at the poem she had just written, Margaret read:

I Had a Dream
One night I dreamed a dream.
I was walking along the beach with my Lord.
Across the dark sky flashed scenes from my life.
For each scene, I noticed two sets
of footprints in the sand,
one belonging to me
and one to my Lord.
When the last scene of my life shot before me
I looked back at the footprints in the sand.
There was only one set of footprints.
I realized that this was at the lowest
and saddest times of my life.

This always bothered me
and I questioned the Lord
about my dilemma.
"Lord, You told me when I decided to follow You,
You would walk and talk with me all the way.
But I'm aware that during the most troublesome
times of my life there is only one set of footprints.
I just don't understand why, when I needed You most,
You leave me."
He whispered, "My precious child,
I love you and will never leave you
never, ever, during your trials and testings.
When you saw only one set of footprints
it was then that I carried you."

Written by Margaret Fishback Powers,
Thanksgiving, 1964, at Echo Lake Youth Camp,
Kingston, Ontario, Canada

For years the poem was falsely ascribed to a little church
mouse named, "Anonymous." Though Margaret is only
4'10" in stature, that is as close to a mouse as she gets.
She lives with her husband Paul in western Canada.
Paul is a children's evangelist and author who published
a heart-rending account of his own abusive upbringing

in his life story, *Too Tough To Cry*. Margaret has raised two daughters, Christina Michelle and Paula Margaret. She is a published poet and author. One book, *Footprints*, is published by HarperCollins Publishers Ltd. A brief personal history of her life, it outlines the true story behind the poem that inspired millions.

When it comes to poetry, Margaret stands tall indeed. In seeking to establish her authorship (to the public) of "I Had a Dream," or, as it is more popularly known, *Footprints*, many unforeseen circumstances got in the way. First of all, her poetry was lost while moving. It was such a terrible feeling to have to prove the authorship of her own work that at one point Margaret almost despaired. But then the solution appeared during a conversation with her mother. As is so often the case, the proof lay close at hand, tucked away in the wedding memorabilia of so many years ago. Margaret's mother reminded her that Footprints had been printed in her Wedding and Bridal albums. Margaret immediately checked and there, sure enough, was the proof she needed. How gratifying to finally be vindicated in the eyes of any who were skeptical!

The *Footprints* book has universal appeal. It is found in bookstores everywhere. Both those within the Christian

Church and those without are captivated by its spiritual appeal. Margaret hears more and more stories of how its inspirational message has helped someone through their moments of crisis. The would-be suicide, the emotionally upset teenager, the widow by the graveside, all attest to the comforting presence of Footprints. Inspired by the outpouring of support, Margaret shares a selection of these letters—with the kind permission of their authors—in the following pages.

Originally, Margaret entitled her poem, "I Had a Dream." In many ways, her original title reflects the divine guidance that alone could explain its popularity and healing effect. Truly, Margaret has captured the essence of the heart's cry when feeling abandoned by both God and man. Her poem seems to make sense out of life's heart-breaking situations having been born itself out of her own heart-rending experience in which only God's love could heal. For many years her authorship went unrecognized, but now she is finally receiving recognition for her inspired work. Her dream has continued to survive, and her marriage and family warmly attest to its reality.

The power of Christ's love once again has shown us that He heals the broken-hearted and makes sense of our periods of sorrow. In the words of another poet, Henry Wadsworth Longfellow (1807-1862):

> Lives of great ones all remind us
>> We can make our lives sublime,
> And, departing, leave behind us
>> Footprints on the sands of time.
>
> Footprints, that perhaps another,
>> Sailing o'er life's solemn main,
> A forlorn and shipwrecked brother,
>> Seeing, shall take heart again.

(from "A Psalm of Life")

Margaret Fishback Powers' poem, Footprints, has achieved that end.

During the past few years, and since the release of *Foot-prints: The True Story Behind the Poem That Inspired Millions*, literally thousands of cards and letters have been forwarded to me from HarperCollins's offices worldwide, letters that express a wide range of thoughts and emotions. Those who wrote had been touched by the poem, Foot-prints, by the book, or by one of the many personal speaking engagements I have made around the world with my missionary evangelist husband, Paul.

While reading and sharing some stories, I found myself feeling like a proud grandparent showing off the snapshots of the grandkids to all who would look and listen. With other stories, having been drawn into the farthest reaches of people's hearts and given the privilege of knowing their intimate and inspirational thoughts, I dared not share them with family or friends, lest I should lose any of that sacred intimacy.

Oftentimes I would pick up my letters and parcels from the mailbox and set out for my favorite coffee shop to read and ponder some serious and heartbreaking stories before moving on to a busy day. Occasionally, I would receive letters that made me smile or chuckle, or even laugh heartily, and a waitress would venture over to my table to see what was going on. I might show her an enclosed photograph and tell her how much it reminded me of our beach walk so many years ago.

Letters kept pouring in and I wanted to share them with the staff of HarperCollins. After much soul searching, and encouragement on their part, I agreed to contact many of those who had written, and to seek their permission to release their special stories to others. I am very pleased that I was not the one to make the final selection of letters for this book, as there were so many heartwarming (and heartfelt) letters that I would have been unable to choose among them.

I am encouraged by the care and respect the editorial staff of HarperCollins, Toronto, Canada have shown in the making of this book. With the multicolored threads of many experiences, they have woven a tapestry so beautiful that the prints of our Lord and Savior are visible throughout. Truly, they have a heart to minister to you, the reader.

Thanks,

Margaret Fishback Powers

FRIENDS OF

Footprints

*O*ne night I dreamed a dream.

I was walking along the beach with my Lord.

Across the dark sky flashed scenes from my life.

Dear Margaret:

What a joy you are! It was really great to have you as our guest in the Crystal Cathedral on Sunday!

Your interview was just fantastic—you light up our lives with your inspiring, uplifting true story! For sure, your words moved us all very deeply, and left a lasting impression in our minds and in our hearts.

Your strong invincible faith comes through in a very powerful way and I know that our millions of viewers will be deeply touched when they hear your message. Indeed, you've helped us all to see the Footprints of God everywhere!

Thanks from the bottom of my heart for sharing with so much forthright simplicity, sincerity and eloquence. This worldwide ministry would not be possible without caring people like you!

With affection and esteem,

Robert H. Schuller
Crystal Cathedral
Garden Grove, California

Dear Mrs. Powers:

I have just finished reading your book *Footprints* and felt compelled to write to you. It wasn't because, like so many others before me, I was strategically moved or affected by your poem, (although this could undoubtedly be said to be the case), but because I have been strategically affected by the book that came about as a result of the frustrations you felt when your poem was plagiarized.

For me, the book has been of far more value at this time in my life than the poem that inspired it. Without the loss of your poem and its subsequent misuse, you probably would never have written the book. It was the book, though, that released me from a burden that has all but crushed the very life out of me for most of my life, depriving me of nearly all my creative power.

When I read the message to your heart in Chapter 18 ("Relinquishment"), I could empathize with every emotion and recognize every stumbling block you identified. I also, for different reasons, had been consumed with a feeling of injustice, and had allowed an unnamed bitterness to suffocate all the life the Lord's spirit had breathed into me. As the months and years passed, my anger grew and my tongue became a two-edged sword, used for hacking any person who dared to hurt me.

Inevitably, my isolation grew, separating me from the benefits of friendships and Christian fellowship, as well as depriving others of what the Lord had given to me to give to others. Yet I could find no way out of my prison.

Just recently I suffered a severe trauma when I fell more than two hundred feet from a deflated paraglider, hitting the side of a hill with such force that I might easily have been killed. Yet I survived, and got away with just minor breaks and bruises. My time in hospital and the weeks since have been more a nightmare of spirit than of body, though, since I have been confronted by all those "imprisoned" phantoms from my past that were released by the trauma. In my agony of spirit, I finally broke down and screamed to the Lord for the particular brand of help that I always thought He was depriving me of for some strange reason—freedom from the enormous and crippling pain in my heart. He had supplied all of my other needs, so why not this one? Accepting God's timetable is the hardest bit for "impatient me" because I don't have His perspective.

On that day of my scream, whilst at my lowest point, I was walking past a Christian bookstore in my nearby shopping center. I hadn't been in the shop for nearly a year and had no reason to go there on that day, but I felt what I can only describe as being irresistibly drawn in. And there, right in front of me as I opened the door, was your book! I don't know why I bought it. Perhaps it was the subject matter. Really, I was expecting little more than another sentimental account of a "born-again" privileged spiritual arrival. Instead, I read a beautiful and candidly honest story of two very human people with whom I could easily identify, and whose story held the answer for which I had searched for so long.

I guess God really does work in some very strange ways. Your original loss has become my priceless gain. Personally speaking, I am glad you lost your boxes with your poems because I now have your book—as do many thousands of other people who need the particular kind of help the Lord is giving through you. I guess we should always remember that everything in our lives is a gift from God, and when we offer it back to Him to use we cannot expect to dictate the terms. Perhaps in the case of your poem He thought you were hanging on too jealously to a message of comfort that He had intended to share with everyone. Perhaps, in the end, He decided to utilize the fast route, one He knew commercialism guaranteed (man's monetary greed is guaranteed to spread a "sure seller" far and wide). Or perhaps He wanted you to write the book I have just read, to reach people like me who needed a little more than can be found from reading just your poem.

I always try to think of my life as being like the loaves and fishes offered to Jesus. If I offer what little I have to Him and trustingly leave it in His hands, He can multiply it beyond my wildest dreams, helping me to achieve goals I had not even imagined He had in mind for me. But if I interfere, or try to take all or part of it back, then apart from depriving others, I remain hungry and ineffective.

Thank you for being willing to stand in the place the Lord has chosen for you.

With love in Christ,

Leicester
England

For the Lord will not cast off for ever: But though he cause grief, yet will he have compassion according to the multitude of his mercies. For he doth not afflict willingly nor grieve the children of men.
Lamentations 3 : 31-33

Dear Mrs. Fishback Powers:

I am writing to you to express how much your poem "I Had a Dream," and your book *Footprints*, have touched me.

About two years ago I was in a Hallmark store and, just by chance, came across the poem Footprints on a sympathy card. I'm not in the habit of browsing in that particular section, and as I was not looking for a sympathy card at the time, it really was just a coincidence that I was introduced to your poem.

I picked up the card and read it. It made me cry. It moved me so much that I bought it. There hadn't been a death or anything, I just thought it was so beautiful that I had to buy it. I showed it to several people. Some had already seen it, but others found it touching, too. I wondered at the "Author Unknown" caption, thinking, "Who wouldn't want to claim responsibility for such a beautiful work?"

It's very important for me to stress to you that I am a young woman of twenty-seven years of age and that I *never* buy sympathy cards unless there has already been a death. I sometimes purchase other types of greeting cards without a specific person in mind, if a card has really touched me, but not sympathy cards. At the time,

I told myself that I would keep the card and give it only to someone that I cared about very much. I felt at the time that such a purchase had certain morbid connotations, but that the power of your words was undeniable.

Last week, on Good Friday, I was in a bookstore with a friend. We were at the checkout counter when I noticed the book *Footprints* on a counter-top display. I picked it up and scanned the front and back covers. It struck me how this poem, which I'd always seen as "Author Unknown" or "Anonymous," was now being claimed by someone. The blurb on the cover said that the book was about how the author came to write the poem. I put the book back, then picked it up again. This went on for a few more moments before I finally decided to buy it as an Easter present for a friend. I was intrigued and wanted to read it too.

My friend Linda, for whom I'd bought the book, is a Christian and has been going through a crisis of faith lately that has caused her great inner turmoil and heartache. I thought that whatever you had to say in your book might certainly be of comfort to her in her personal struggles.

At Easter, while visiting my folks, I showed them your book. An amazing thing happened. My father, who has *never* read a book in his life (except when he was in school), asked me to lend it to him when I had finished it.

I gave the book to Linda and told her how you wrote of dealing with some incredible struggles, and how the poem came to be. She was very pleased. I'm sure, in her time of confusion, that she will derive some notion of peace and faith such as she once had until so very recently. I have asked her to lend the book to my Dad when she's done.

Recently, I was in another card shop and saw your poem on a plate with your name at the bottom. I felt so pleased. I saw it in French as well, since we live in Quebec. It's sort of a hobby now to see if credit is given where it is due.

I simply wanted to tell you how you touched my life and how comforting I have found your words to be. Thank you for your wonderful gift. You have touched so many people.

Sincerely,

Kelly
Quebec

Peace I leave with you, my peace I give unto you: not as the world giveth, give I unto you. Let not your heart be troubled, and neither let it be afraid.

St. John 14 : 27

I just finished reading your book, *Footprints*, and had this overwhelming desire to talk to you, even if it's only through writing. This is a first for me, but I know that if it is of the Lord, He will see to it that we communicate.

First, I must tell you that what little I learned of you through *Footprints* has given me great admiration and respect for you. I feel as though I know you in a teacher/ student sort of way. I believe the Lord has blessed you with great wisdom, insight and understanding. You have that intimacy with our Lord that I so desire. At the same time, I know it comes with great responsibility to Him and others. That frightens me.

Thank you for being so obedient to the Lord and for publishing your book. Also, I believe you were very wise in the Lord for not taking action against those people for publishing your poems. The Lord will greatly reward you for that.

I wanted to tell you how much your poems mean to me, especially "Letter from a Friend." I've had that plaque for a good while, but one day a few years ago I neglected my relationship with the Lord—badly. One day when I was cleaning house (I always dust the pic- tures on the walls), well, I got to that plaque and for some reason I stopped to read it. It was as though God took me by the shoulders and just shook me to get my attention. It had such a profound effect on me. It touched me in a very special way. Thank you. Thank you for allowing God to use you in this way because your poems have touched many lives.

Sincerely in Christ,

Terry
Texas

For whosoever shall do the will of my Father which is in heaven, the same is my brother, and sister, and mother.
St. Matthew 12 : 50

Dear Margaret:

In late 1981 or '82 the poem Footprints was given to me. I can't remember either who gave it to me or under what circumstances, but thought that since it was typed in the sign of the cross the poem would be special. I gave a copy to one of my born-again friends and to an Irish lady. Both made photocopies and passed them on as gifts. One year later my friend was enthusiastically greeted by a man who thrust a paper into her hand and said, "You must have this!" Sure enough, it was a copy of the poem I had passed around the year before, typed on my typewriter in the sign of the cross. My Irish friend sent copies to Ireland, and each of her friends there passed copies throughout Europe.

My dear, what goes around comes around, and now eleven years later I can happily say that I have had the privilege of writing to you and thanking you for letting me know that God has carried me too. I would like you to know that some people come into our lives and leave footprints on our hearts, and we are never ever the same.

With sincere gratitude,

Susan
New York

Know therefore that the Lord thy God, he is God; the faithful God, which keepeth covenant and mercy with them that love him and keep his commandments to a thousand generations.

Deuteronomy 7 : 9

Dear Margaret:

Thank you for writing that poem Footprints. It has
given me strength many times. Once you've read it, you
don't forget it.

God works in so many wondrous ways—our thoughts
and ideas are so far from His and yet He uses us. I guess,
had it not been for Paul's faith in God, he wouldn't
have told you God would carry you both when the troubled waters came, and you wouldn't have penned the
poem. I pray that God will give you the courage to put
more of your poems down on paper, and to have them
published so that they will inspire others to take a closer
walk and to turn to the Bible for a greater faith and
knowledge to serve Him.

Maybe this "thank you" note is a bit like a royalty
payment. I know it won't pay the phone bills, but
maybe if you get a million letters like this they will give
you the inspiration and strength to go on, as you with

your poem have given others the inspiration and strength to go on.

In Christ,

Marian
Alberta

For ye know the grace of our Lord Jesus Christ, that, though he was rich, yet for your sakes he became poor, that ye through his poverty might be rich.

II Corinthians 8 : 9

Dear Margaret:

One of my sons gave me your book, *Footprints*, as a Christmas present. He couldn't have chosen a better gift. Both my wife and I have read it with great interest, for the poem has a special place in our memories.

Five years ago I was stricken with a virus that collapsed my lungs and punctured them both in seven or eight places. This resulted in me spending one month in Intensive Care, two months in the General ward at the hospital and a year at home on oxygen. I am not fully recovered, but my blood now has the capacity to make oxygen at 80 percent efficiency, so I operate reasonably well.

When I came out of Intensive Care and was lying in my private room, I had a visit from the surgeon who had operated on me a few times. This fellow may well have been a fine surgeon, but he was totally lacking in human skills. I still remember one operation that he did while I was partially conscious and scared. He told me, standing in the doorway, that if the leaks in my lungs didn't heal themselves within two months, he would have to operate again. My specialist and GP hadn't told me about this as they were concentrating on building a positive attitude to help the healing process. I was frightened and did not know how I could handle the situation—and then I remembered a poem that a friend had given me that very afternoon. It was your poem. I read it again and the answer came to me. I then talked to God and told him that because I was incapable of worrying about future operations and building a positive attitude at the same time, I would leave the future to Him and would concentrate instead on being positive each day. Having had this talk and made this decision, I relaxed, for I knew that He would "carry me."

Two months later, the surgeon appeared again and commented on the fact that I still had one leak in a lung that had not healed. He said that he would therefore have to operate the following week! That night I talked to God and pointed out that He had done a fine job of healing, but that He now would have to go into high gear or my worst fear would come true.

I awakened the next morning as usual, while the nurse was inspecting the bottle containing the fluids still leaking from my lung. In fact, I awoke rather quickly because she said, "It's stopped leaking!" I couldn't believe it and neither could she, since the leaks always sealed themselves off gradually over the period of a week or more and this one had just stopped—period. When the specialist came in later that day, he examined the drainage bottle and said that there must be a blockage somewhere, and left instructions for a resident doctor to inspect the attachment to my body. Result? Nothing wrong! After a week of waiting, the doctors decided that "for some reason" the leak had healed itself and I could go home, without any further surgery!

I have since had a friend write your poem in calligraphy, and have given framed copies to all my children. Of course, I have the original on the wall of our guest bedroom.

Thank you, Margaret, for writing that poem. It has certainly been a great comfort to me. I have now inscribed your name on the back of the framed copy.

Paul
Alberta

Why art thou cast down, O my soul? and why art thou
disquieted within me? hope thou in God: for I shall yet praise Him,
who is the health of my countenance, and my God.

Psalm 42 : 11

Dear Mrs. Powers:

I recently received a gift from my wife Betty—your book. We are both avid readers and she is well aware of how I feel about Footprints. It is one of the most inspirational pieces written by anyone, ever.

That kind of work, to me, is like a Mona Lisa. It can never be duplicated, only admired.

I am writing this letter for two reasons. The first is to add my name to the list of millions who have read and been inspired by Footprints. The second reason has two parts. First, I would like to congratulate you on your book. It too is inspirational and does a lot to explain the inspiration behind Footprints. Second, I too write, mostly for my own enjoyment and for that of my family and friends.

I want you to know that through Footprints and through your book, you have made the world a little better place and that is the goal, I believe, each Christian should have.

God bless you,

Louis
Michigan

For if these things be in you, and abound, they make you that ye shall neither be barren nor unfruitful in the knowledge of our Lord Jesus Christ.

II Peter 1 : 8

Dear Margaret:

I have been a singer/songwriter for most of my life. I have released two country albums in Canada and Europe, written and co-written with Nashville writers, and have performed in concert and on TV and radio. But nothing excited me more than the chance to be a part of a project as world-renowned as Footprints. I must thank God and you for the opportunity to be involved in such a wonderful and world-famous piece of art. This is truly an honour.

I set to work immediately. For more than a year I tried and tried to come up with a song form that could do justice to Footprints, but nothing seemed to work. I just couldn't find the right ingredients to turn Footprints into a song. Talk about a lesson in frustration.

I put my tape recorder, paper, pen and your poem on our kitchen table and sat looking at the empty page. I'd already tried every way I knew to make this song. Now what was I going to do?

So one morning, by myself in my kitchen, I put my pen down and silently asked, "Lord, I don't know how to do this, I could sure use some help on this one."

This is how Footprints became a song—after trying and trying by myself, I know God carried me.

Rocky
British Columbia

Now faith is the substance of things hoped for, the evidence of things not seen.

Hebrews 11 : 1

Dear Paul and Margaret:

Hi there! I am writing to you from in front of a cozy wood stove fire in my farmhouse kitchen in Quebec. The snow is falling softly outside on a beautiful Gatineau Hills landscape.

Thanks to both of you, my/our collection of special books has significantly increased recently! My family will greatly appreciate these wonderful gifts at Christmas next week. Of course, I am extremely grateful to both of you for your thoughtful generosity!

Enclosed, you will find a print of my holiday message to all of the Informatics staff of the RCMP across Canada. I've also enclosed several copies of the prints I made of Margaret's poem for you.

Already I have received a great deal of positive feedback! I will also give a copy to the RCMP Commissioner, Phil Murray, who I know will greatly appreciate it.

You are wonderful people! We'll keep in touch!

May God bless your family!

Steve
Quebec

P.S.: My daughter Julie just arrived home from university. She was a bit disappointed to hear that a human being had actually written Footprints. Nothing personal, Margaret, but she had always believed that an *angel* had written the beautiful poem! I told her that she can still hold onto that belief—because Margaret is an angel!

All scripture is given by inspiration of God, and is profitable for doctrine, for reproof, for correction, for instruction in righteousness: that the man of God may be perfect, thoroughly furnished unto all good works.
II Timothy 3 : 16–17

For each scene, I noticed two sets

of footprints in the sand,

one belonging to me

and one to my Lord.

When the last scene of my life shot before me

I looked back at the footprints in the sand.

There was only one set of footprints.

Dear Margaret:

We went for a picnic on August 7, 1989, with three other families. It was a beautiful sunny day. This was the first time we had gone to Golden Ears Park since moving to Vancouver. We left the park around 2:30 p.m., and on the way home we saw some ambulances going into the park. We all wondered what had happened. Since I had read the book *Footprints*, I knew what had happened on that day. It was like reading a storybook, and this was just a miracle. God had done a wonderful thing for the Powers' family.

It was in the hospital, while looking after my brother, that I first read the poem Footprints. In 1982 my brother was very ill, suffering from both lung and bone cancer. He had been in the hospital for a while and was under radiotherapy treatment. He suffered a lot from the illness, and the treatment made him very weak. When I read the poem, I was deeply touched by it and felt the presence of God's love and also His care for His children. Since then I have loved the poem, and every time I read it I am comforted by it.

Dear Margaret, I am still learning to forgive and forget, and also to leave it with the Lord. It is not easy to learn this, but I know that everything is in God's hands. He is the potter and I am the clay.

In Christ,

Inge
British Columbia

The Lord also will be a refuge for the oppressed, a refuge in times of trouble.

Psalm 9 : 9

Dear Mrs. Powers:

Hi! I just finished reading your book about the poem "I
Had a Dream." A non-Christian friend of mine showed
it to me and I remember thinking, "Hey! That's cool!"
The whole idea of your poem helped make Jesus more
real to me. The concept you introduced has helped me
to accept my life as Jesus directs it. I now know how to
trust in Him. After reading your book, I have learned to
be more thankful for what I have and who I am.

In His Hands,

Jessica
Alabama

*He that hath my commandments, and keepeth them, he it is that
loveth me: and he that loveth me shall be loved of my Father, and I
will love him, and will manifest myself to him.*

St. John 14 : 21

Dear Margaret:

I received my first copy of Footprints in the mail. Although I didn't realize it then, this was a turning point in my life.

I was never in a hurry to read our monthly church bulletin because I was always on the go. When I finally did and came to the Footprints poem, I became very still as I read. I was so moved that by the time I reached the end I was weeping. It was as if the world stood still for a few moments, for this beautiful poem penetrated to my inner soul. I remember thinking that I knew this poem, it was so familiar, but perhaps it was my soul that knew and remembered God, for we are all spiritual beings having a human experience.

Footprints contributed to my spiritual awakening, but I hadn't been ready to accept God into my life until Footprints came along. A transformation occurred. I went from being a self-centered, ego-minded person who never showed emotion, to one who let her tears flow freely both in joy and sorrow and always with God. Years later, I finally learned the meaning of humility.

Through the years I have read many "nice" anonymous poems. The fact that they were anonymous didn't seem to bother me. When I first read Footprints, however,

I was disappointed when I saw that there was no author. I knew someone had to have written the original poem. I thought perhaps it had been written during Christ's time here on Earth. I pictured one of the disciples walking with Jesus by the river Jordan, leaving his footprints in the sand. Still, I always wondered who, where and when. Such a precious poem and so eloquently written! I felt that whoever the author was must have had enough faith to move mountains.

A few of us went to see my Aunt Mary, who was dying of cancer in Burnaby General Hospital. I was the one chosen to read Footprints to her. Once again the world stood still for those few minutes. I remember hearing my voice so clear, as if someone else were reading. I was trying so hard to keep strong and to not cry. Suddenly we all felt a certain peace that linked us together. Footprints was to remain forever in our hearts.

From that moment on, Footprints gave our family the faith and courage to go on, and to let God carry us when we needed it. Aunt Mary found her peace and suffered no more. She passed away thirty minutes after midnight, the night of my thirtieth birthday. Footprints became my special poem, and I gave a copy to all those near and dear to my heart.

I thought that was it, but not even a month later I

was drawn to look at "The Friendship Book of Francis Gay." I looked up the reading for my birthday and couldn't believe it—it was Footprints. Out of 365 days, the author picked my birthday, November 13, to include this poem!

It seemed that this poem was suddenly everywhere, leaping out at me and in some of the strangest places. God was shouting, "Wake up, don't you know that I'm here for you?" It was like God was hitting me over the head, trying to knock some spiritual sense into me. Footprints came in many forms—bookmarks, calendars, wall clocks, and plaques. The most appropriate form, I thought, was on sympathy cards and "thinking of you" cards. Most of the time it would say "Author Unknown." All of a sudden I started seeing people's names under my special poem, and I would become so angry. How dare they put their name under my special poem? How dare they steal and claim something so precious as their own? How could they sleep at night? It was like they were stealing from God. Didn't they know that whatever they did to others would come back to them? I refused to accept anyone falsely claiming to be the author, and would never buy anything unless it said "Anonymous" or "Author Unknown."

For the past several years, Footprints has followed me

everywhere. It became the spiritual guide that helped me stay on the right path with God, and was always a reminder that God was with me. Still, I never stopped wondering who the actual author was. I remember going to a Sunday service and talking about Footprints. My timing was excellent, as one lady said, "Wasn't the true author discovered?" Then another one remembered. I was told that the true author had been found and was alive and well. I went to the library, found the newspaper article, read it and in my heart and soul I knew— Margaret Fishback Powers was the true author.

I remember thinking, I must make enough copies to let everyone know. I mailed and circulated many copies. I sent a copy to a friend in North Carolina and was so surprised when she replied on Footprints stationery. There was Margaret's name, right there where it belonged! My friend had had this stationery for a few years, but until I wrote to her she didn't know that Margaret was the true author.

It seemed that October, the month Footprints was originally written (in 1964), had become my month for Footprints as well because it was in October 1993 that I finally learned the name of the true author.

Today I know that nothing happens by coincidence. There is a reason for everything. I know that it is not what happens to me that is important, but what I do with what happens. Today, I know how to put God first in my life—to wake up with "Good morning, God" instead of "Good God, it's morning!" When those trying times are there, I have learned to "Let go and let God." No matter what, I now have faith and trust in God, for He is my very best friend.

Footprints has been my spiritual journey. It has been a slow but steady climb upwards. I can't even remember how it felt to have a shallow and empty life. Footprints represents my Aunt Mary, her strength and her belief, as well as my spiritual awakening, my life, love, faith, strength and the footprints we all leave behind when we pass on.

Catherine
British Columbia

Now our Lord Jesus Christ himself, and God, even our Father, which hath loved us, and hath given us everlasting consolation and good hope through grace, Comfort your hearts, and stablish you in every good word and work.

II Thessalonians 2 : 16–17

Dear Margaret:

I have just finished reading your book *Footprints: The True Story Behind The Poem That Inspired Millions* and felt a compelling need to write to you.

About four years ago, as a non-Christian, I came across a plate in a gift shop in a seaside town while on holiday. On the plate was printed the poem Footprints, and I was moved to tears then and there thinking how lovely it would be to believe it.

Just one year ago Jesus called me to follow Him. I was saved quite suddenly and quite dramatically. Oh, how my life has changed! The peace and joy I have found! As a new Christian one of my new-found friends gave me a bookmark with the poem Footprints printed on it. I cannot tell you how moving and comforting it is. I keep it in my Bible and read it often. Then, on the day of my baptism, the same friend gave me your book.

The point of my letter is this: although I can understand how upset you were when your poems went missing and then turned up again, they have reached a far wider public like this than they would have done had they been tucked away in a book in a Christian bookstore.

Praise the Lord that His word, through your hand,

has managed to reach so many people, Christian and non-Christian, more than you probably thought possible. You should be very proud and take great comfort that God's will, not yours, has been done.

Irene
Essex, England

For then shalt thou have thy delight in the Almighty, and shalt lift up thy face unto God.

Job 22 : 26

Dear Margaret:

Although I have no right to call you "Dear Margaret" because we have never met, I feel as though somehow we are kindred spirits. What has prompted me to write this letter is the completion of your *Footprints* book. I feel I must share how much this poem has meant to me over the past eleven years.

My name is Diane and I am a single parent with two beautiful children (David and Melissa). We live in Alberta. As I read your book this evening, I wept with a prayer of thanks for your writing the Footprints poem. You see, eleven years ago my husband met another woman and moved out to marry her, leaving me alone with two children of eighteen months and three and one-half years of age. During my two-year recovery period from the shock, I met a wonderful man who wanted to marry me. I too wished to be his wife, but was not ready yet to say yes because I did not want to drag my "baggage" into a new relationship. So I kept asking him to be patient with me until my healing work was done. I did not, however, anticipate that he would one day give up asking me and move away! How I related to your reservations about saying yes to Paul at his proposal! Although I have had much loss and many trials in my life, never had I known the grief I felt during that time. And while I was grieving, my two best friends became ill with cancer. Both died within the following two years.

It was during this time that I discovered the Footprints poem. I immediately bought one copy for myself and others for friends in pain too.

I remember so vividly the day that I decided to share *your* poem with my church, in a response to sharing what Christmas meant to me. You see, I had slipped into such a deep depression that I had become numb and this turned into the toughest battle of my life. More than anything, I wanted to die to stop the pain. Every day, for two solid years, I woke up with thoughts of suicide. I truly thought my children would be better off without this depressed and broken role model of a mother! Something deep inside me made me reach out, and through a "generic" twelve-step program and your poem, I made it through this devastating healing time. When I read your poem to our congregation at Christmas 1989, I shared a part of this time in my life and how I had come to surrender my life into God's hands. You see, I was not brought up in a Christian home and my early experience with Christianity was terrifying to me through a very "army approach" (which left out the loving part of God!). I turned away from what little I had understood about God, until my father died in 1971. Because I was so angry at God for taking this wonderful man, I came to realize that I must believe! So it has been an interesting twenty-plus years' journey in allowing God into my heart.

May God bless you with much joy in coming years, and may you continue to share your gift of writing with the world—the world hungers for your God-given grace on paper!

Diane
Alberta

And not only so, but we glory in tribulations also:
knowing that tribulation worketh patience;
And patience, experience; and experience, hope.

Romans 5 : 3–4

Dear Margaret:

I just finished reading your book *Footprints*. I must say it greatly moved me. The love and faith you have for God are what I have been struggling to find for many years. I am Christian in name, but not in spirit. Reading your book has filled me with an inspiration I cannot describe; God is truly with you in many ways.

A few months ago, trying to find God, I started reading the Bible. I feel a void in my life I am not sure how to fill. I thought the Bible would have the answers; it didn't. All I felt when I read the Bible was disbelief that a non-human could create all we know today. To me, this was not logical. Did you ever have grave doubts as to whether or not God was watching over you? There are many things that have troubled me in the past couple of months that make it hard to believe that God is always there watching us. Why does He put us through these "trials and testings?" I have so many questions I need to ask but am not sure where to find the answers. Could you help me?

For the past seven years I have been attending a center run by the United Church of Canada. This place is my Heaven on Earth. It is a community with a loving and accepting atmosphere where I have always felt welcome and secure. Last year I experienced a spiritual need to find and talk to God, yet I have never known where to find Him. I know I feel Him in the music I hear, but it is just not enough. I want more. I want to feel God in everything I do. Your book has provided me with the motivation to start searching for God. I want to recover my "wholeness of heart," as you have done.

In your book you have expressed some situations that are similar to my own. I often feel a bitterness towards the actions of others, but I am unable to express this strong and upsetting emotion. Your story touched my heart. Thank you for writing it. Even though published illegally, "I Had a Dream" has inspired many, especially myself, and for that I thank you. If you are still doing talks to people of your knowledge of and faith in God, I would love to come and hear you.

Thank you sincerely and graciously,

Angela
British Columbia

And ye shall seek me, and find me when ye shall search for me with all your heart.

Jeremiah 29 : 13

Dear Margie:

Hi! My name is Mary Beth and I'm writing to say "thank you" for sharing your story of Footprints, especially Chapter 18: "Relinquishment." As one of God's many messengers, you brought to me His love and understanding just when I needed it most. It is a powerful and healing message. God brought me to you to share in this message in an amazing way.

Being the wife of a professional tractor trailer driver, I often travel with my husband. On two separate occasions the word "powers" was written on a shower faucet in a truck stop, to get my attention. Knowing that "powers" is the fourth order of angels, I knew a message was forthcoming.

The morning after the second occasion, we stopped for fuel. I went inside to freshen up, telling my husband I would meet him at the fuel desk. As I waited, I noticed a bookrack and was drawn to it. I reached for a book hidden behind another and when I saw the author's name, your name, I thought there may be something in it for me. My husband too is aware of the angels. I showed him the book and we were off, book in hand. Between the bumps and by the next afternoon, I had finished reading it. Chapter 18 has had a profound effect on me. I cried a lot while reading it and struggled to see through my tears. I realized, with the help of Noah Webster, that the "big debt" was the bitterness I have been carrying around all these years (bitter meaning "at great cost") and that in order to "forgive and forget" I have to let it go and give it to God. The bitterness was caused by abusive parents, primarily my mother. I have not been able to let it go, as she is still doing the things she did from years ago. But now, after reading your story, I am willing to give it to God and let Him handle it.

And so, Margie, thank you again with all my heart, and thanks to God and His angels who brought us together.

Mary Beth
Pennsylvania

But love ye your enemies, and do good, and lend, hoping for nothing again; and your reward shall be great, and ye shall be the children of the Highest: for he is kind unto the unthankful and to the evil. Be ye therefore merciful, as your Father also is merciful.
St. Luke 6 : 35–36

Dear Margaret Powers:

I recently read about your authorship of the Footprints poem and felt compelled to tell you how much it changed my life. I have always thanked God for that poem, and now I can thank you.

I first encountered Footprints as a song on a cassette tape when I was heartbroken and in despair over an unfaithful husband. The words so moved and inspired me that I committed them to paper so I could refer to them whenever I felt down or unable to go on with life. I don't know if I would have made it through without them! Several wonderful friends became aware of my "lifesaver" and soon I had Footprints hanging on my wall as a beautifully framed poster, on wallet cards and on desk paperweights. I cherish them all to this day. I have since become a devout Christian, and I still read Footprints whenever I feel the need to strengthen my faith in God in times of trouble.

I understand from the article that you became "angry and bitter" about your poem being published without permission from or credit to you, the author. But for me, it was God's providence. Since the poem was anonymous, it was as if God wrote it to me, personally. I felt He was talking directly to me by creating, apparently from nowhere, this immensely uplifting and faith-building message. Thank you for writing it, and I thank God that He has found a way to touch so many lives with it (especially mine!)

God bless you,

Cathy
Texas

As ye have therefore received Christ Jesus the Lord, so walk ye in him: Rooted and built up in him, and stablished in the faith, as ye have been taught, abounding therein with thanksgiving.

Colossians 2 : 6–7

Dear Mrs. Powers:

I have, in the past five minutes, finished reading your book concerning the history of "I Had a Dream" or Footprints. I could not put your book down after I picked it up, and read it in just over two hours. These past two hours have been another trip to the mountain-top of Peace.

I would like to relate to you my experience with the beautiful poem that God entrusted to you. I was on transfer from National Defence headquarters to the naval base at Esquimalt. During the drive out west I visited with my sister near Edmonton. On her dining room wall hung a copy of your poem. I was instantly taken by the beauty of its imagery. I asked my sister to mail me a copy of it should she ever find it in another store. I was not a practising Christian at this time but I had been raised with a Christian background. I stopped going to church about the same time you wrote this work.

After arriving in Esquimalt, a package arrived from my sister with my first copy of Footprints in it. I took great pleasure in hanging it in my dining room and read it daily. A few weeks after I hung it over my dining room table, a close friend experienced the tragic loss of his wife due to an aneurysm in her brain. My friend was devastated and began a grieving process that made him drink very heavily. One night he wrecked his car and almost killed himself in the process. I, along with the rest of his friends, was becoming very concerned for his safety. One evening as I ate my evening meal, I looked at Footprints and the answer came to me. I took Footprints down and walked over to my friend's house, not sure what I was going to say or if I'd still have this friend when I returned home. I went into his kitchen and told him to sit down and listen to me. I voiced my concerns for him, and then gave him the copy of Footprints and left. That was ten years ago. My friend is remarried and very happy. Above his bed hangs my first copy of Footprints.

It would be enough if the story ended there, but that was only the beginning. As you are well aware, God moves in mysterious and wonderful ways. Footprints was the beginning of a personal spiritual odyssey that led me to a new career. This September I begin studies and with the grace of God will be ordained to holy orders in about three years' time. The road I have travelled to come this far has been scattered with obstacles and periods of deep questioning. Through it all, when times looked the bleakest, Footprints has reminded me of the support and love that God gives us so freely. And now thanks to your wonderful work, I have another reminder to look towards when times get tough: "Leave it there." I was moved to tears reading this, especially since I am trying to deal with an obstacle that could prevent me from attending school in the fall. "Leave it there" has helped to remove this burden.

Your Servant in Christ,

Sandy
Saskatchewan

And I will bring the blind by a way that they knew not; I will lead them in paths that they have not known: I will make darkness light before them, and crooked things straight. These things will I do unto them, and not forsake them.

Isaiah 42 : 16

I realized that this was at the lowest

and saddest times of my life.

This always bothered me

and I questioned the Lord

about my dilemma.

Dear Margaret:

My brother, Jay, two friends from our church (Derek and Rick) and I had gone up for a plane ride in a four-seater Cessna—my very first plane trip! Nearing the runway for our descent, the little plane's engine stalled and it nosedived into the dense thicket of trees in a ravine. Jay, Derek and Rick were killed instantly. Four days later I awakened in the hospital just when the triple funeral at our church was taking place. I awakened with severe memory loss, a severely damaged ankle and awful damage to my face.

As I recovered, I struggled to recall my brother, yet I couldn't remember a thing—his appearance, our times together, his laughter. I had lost him and even my memory of him. I was just turning seventeen. I was fifteen when the Cessna came down.

As I record this story, I still don't remember his face and I still can't hear his voice. I can't remember the times we spent together, but I still remember the love and care I had for him and the comfort I felt when I was with him. That is something that has always been there and always will be, and I thank God for that.

I was in the hospital for about a month before I started recalling things and holding them in my memory. A nurse describing this experience to my mom compared it to picking up files that had been scattered. She said it would take time, perhaps even two years, before all the files were back in order.

I got out of the hospital on crutches on October 31, so Halloween had a completely different meaning for my family and, I think, for our youth group. When I came home from the hospital there was a big flashing sign in our yard saying, "Welcome home Karla," and my whole youth group and other friends were at my house to welcome me home. I will never forget that! God has blessed me with a lot of good friends and a strong church family. Through them God carried us.

Struggling with bitterness was a subconscious thing. At the time I didn't want to deal with that. I catch myself occasionally thinking about what a great guy Jay was, how much he had to offer, and how much he was loved by so many people. He had great gifts academically and socially. He was brilliant. He could have been any-thing he wanted to be, anything he set his mind to because he was so gifted in every area. He was involved in concert and stage bands and in a rock and roll band— he had so many friends. Why Jay? Why not me? It is hard to describe God's answer to that question, but He did answer me and He does answer me all the time in a still, quiet voice. He says, "Just trust me." I just trust Him and He fills me with an incredible peace that I can't describe. If that's what trusting Him does, I want to trust Him more! I don't think I could ever trust Him enough; I will always be striving to trust Him more!

In the pastor's recent sermon, he mentioned that a person has more impact on someone else after they have been taken away than they do when they are alive. When Jay was alive, I don't ever recall thanking God for him by saying, "Thank you for my brother, he is such a wonderful guy." He was a wonderful guy, but I never consciously acknowledged that or told it to Jay. I thank God for the time we had together. He's the one who made me laugh and helped me to make other people laugh; wherever Jay was there was laughter. I thank God for that laughter in my life. When I remember Jay and his lopsided grin, I laugh, because that was who Jay was. Jay would want me to laugh.

My mom has told me that for a long time she couldn't open her Bible. "How could God permit this? What kind of loving God would allow this to happen to two families who served God faithfully?" She had to take time to work through these questions, but she did work through them and has come out the better for it. But God spared me that. He blessed me with not having to deal with that. It wasn't until the shock was over that there was time for me to think about Jay. My thoughts initially had all been for myself. God showed Himself as my Preserver, Healer and Comforter from the very beginning. I could see Him only as a gracious and loving God. So if you want an opinion from someone who thinks of God as a cruel God, don't ask me, because I don't know a cruel God. My focus has been on God's love and His grace. It is amazing how His sovereignty, wisdom, grace and mercy all work together, and I thank God for keeping my focus on the Lord Jesus Christ.

Today, I do still struggle with the loss of memory, my limitations, and the bitterness I catch myself feeling. When I find myself feeling that way, the grace of God sees me through and will continue to see me through. It was God's mercy that saved my life and His mercy that healed my ankle to the extent that I now have full movement in it, although I can't participate in any jumping sports. Ironically enough, it is God's grace that has taken my memory from me. I think if I could remember Jay's face and the sound of his voice, and the crash itself, I would have some traumatic emotional damage, but God doesn't allow anything to happen to us that we cannot bear. He says that He will also see us through anything he brings to us, all the way. He has been merciful in doing just that.

I think about these three young men and the love of life that they had and I only hope I will come to enjoy life as much as the three of them did, and that I will come to the deep understanding of God that they had. My desire is the same as theirs: to live life to the fullest for God. I know now, and it has been made very clear to me, that we don't know the number of our days. Only God knows that, so we have to live life to the very fullest, with the understanding that everything will be for our good: "All things work together for good to them that love God." I thank God for this promise and I pray that I will never waste a minute of my life doing other than what God has called me to do. I want to live my life for Him.

Karla (university student)
Ontario

For thou wilt light my candle: the Lord my God will enlighten my darkness.

Psalm 18 : 28

Dear Margaret:

In May of 1987, God saw fit to take home our four-month-old baby son. It was during that time a very close friend of mine sent me the reading Footprints. Footprints became my confirmation that God would not leave me when I so desperately needed Him. My husband and I read that little poem literally hundreds of times, as a reminder to us that God's mighty hand was at work. We believed that God would somehow mend our broken hearts, dry our falling tears and rebuild our lives so that we could continue to serve Him. My special thanks to you, Margie, for allowing God to inspire these precious words in your heart.

Love in Christ,

Kelvin and Leah
New Brunswick

When thou passest through the waters, I will be with thee; and through the rivers, they shall not overflow thee: when thou walkest through the fire, thou shalt not be burned; neither shall the flame kindle upon thee.

Isaiah 43 : 2

Dear Margaret,

It was with a heavy heart that I phoned a dear niece who lives in the small village of Icomb, Stow-on-the-Wold, Gloucester, England, just one week ago today, August 16, 1995. A few days earlier, her eldest bachelor son of twenty-six years of age had been killed in a motorcycle accident. Words of comfort don't come easily when trying to console a distraught mother.

During our conversation, she remarked that instead of sending out the usual "thank-you for your love and deep sympathy" cards, she had purchased a fine quality notepaper with "Footprints in the Sand," the verse which had given great comfort to her at this time.

My niece was surprised when I informed her that in less than a week I would be having dinner with the lady who wrote the inspired Footprints. I live six thousand miles from England, but hearts were lifted at the wonder of God's perfect timing. Only He could have done this, knowing the ache we had and the comfort the poem would bring.

Sincerely,

Ella
British Columbia

Come unto me, all ye that labor and are heavy laden, and I will give you rest.

St. Matthew 11 : 28

Dear Mrs. Powers:

My husband, at thirty-two years of age, was killed in a helicopter crash in 1984. A couple of days later I received a framed copy of your poem as a birthday gift. It had been mailed before the accident. I don't think that was a coincidence. Your words brought great comfort to me at a time when my faith was sorely tested. I cannot say that I never had doubts after that, but every time I read your poem, it moves me to tears.

Sincerely

Karen
Virginia

I will turn their mourning into joy, and will comfort them and make them rejoice from their sorrow.

Jeremiah 31 : 13

Dear Mrs. Powers:

I hope this note reaches you. I just felt I needed to share with you how special your poem is to me and my family.

My beloved mother died just five weeks ago. Your poem was given to her by a special friend some years earlier. This friend was dying of cancer and your poem had been her support.

At my mother's funeral, my cousin read your poem. A feeling of peace and tranquillity passed over us all. I was looking for something special for Dad and discovered our local Christian shop had only one copy of your book left. So again its words will be our support over this special Christmas. I know my mother has gone to a special place with our Lord. My faith has been tested, but renewed.

Thank you for sharing with our family, and the world, these comforting words.

God bless you. With kindest regards,

Jan
England

For the sufferings of Christ abound in us, so our consolation also aboundeth by Christ.

II Corinthians 1 : 5

Dear Margaret:

I learned that my uncle Orland was dying. In fact, his time remaining was so short that a letter might not even reach him in time. I was in Canada and he was in Ohio. I sat down to write, but what do you write to someone who is dying? Especially someone you have never really gotten to know?

The last time I had seen my uncle was nearly ten years ago at the only family reunion our family ever had. It was a wonderful get-together! My three uncles had taken some of us cousins on a tour of the old home places and the old schoolhouse and the little church with its cemetery. My mother, their only sister, had died many years ago when I was just a little girl. I sensed a special bond with my uncle Orland at a particular moment when his eyes met mine. I wondered if he was seeing his "Sis" in me and something about him reminded me of my mother. He was a quiet man and let his brothers do the talking. He had been a widower for many years and had no children.

Now I sat, full of regrets for not having got to know him better, wondering what I could write that might possibly comfort and encourage him. "Lord, please help me know what to write," I prayed, and immediately the poem

Footprints popped into my mind. I didn't have a copy so I wrote the meaning of the poem in my own words.

I wrote that the Lord walks hand in hand with us throughout our lives. Looking back, we can see the two sets of footprints, but during the tough times when we see only one set of footprints, it is not that He has left us, but that the Lord has carried us. I told my uncle that I knew the Lord was carrying him through this tough time in his life.

I learned later that my letter did reach him in time. He was quite touched by the letter and was surprised that he had never heard the poem before! That night he kept asking his nephew to read my letter over and over. Through the long night he reviewed the events of his own life and thought of the people he wanted to ask for forgiveness. Finally, around dawn, he said, "I'm ready now for the Lord to carry me."

Many people from the community came to his funeral. They came to pay tribute to this quiet and good man. Remarks heard over and over were about how honest and big-hearted he was: "He could always be trusted," and, "He was the best auto mechanic in the whole state!" Because the poem Footprints had touched my uncle so profoundly, it was used by the minister in the funeral sermon. Whether my uncle had realized it

or not, the Lord had been walking with him all the days
of his life.

Marilyn
British Columbia

*For this is good and acceptable in the sight of God our Saviour;
Who will have all men to be saved, and to come unto the
knowledge of the truth.*

I Timothy 2 : 3–4

Dear Mrs. Powers:

I received a copy of your book *Footprints* from a dear friend of mine. I love it!

Eleven years ago my daughter died at three months of age from SIDS. She had been a perfectly healthy child and very much loved by me.

My grandmother sent me a framed copy of Footprints, Author Unknown. I've treasured your work for the past eleven years. It led me back with heartache to my Father, who has healed me emotionally and spiritually. I gladly relinquished all my rights to my daughter and rejoice in her happiness in Heaven.

I have had your full name painted onto my framed picture of Footprints.

God bless you,

Jodi
Indiana

They that sow in tears shall reap in joy. He that goeth forth and weepeth, bearing precious seed, shall doubtless come again with rejoicing, bringing his sheaves with him.
Psalm 126 : 5–6

This letter was sent originally to Joni Earickson Tada, author of *Her Story*, *A Step Further*, and *Choices . . . Changes*. Mike, who wrote the letter, later copied it to Margaret.

*   *   *

Dear Joni:

Today in British Columbia I had the most wonderful day anyone could imagine. My wife and I met with Margie and Paul Powers after a really neat set of circumstances. We shared many thoughts and some lunch. During this time I told them how in 1981 I broke my neck in an auto accident in Australia. This event was to reshape my life in the following thirteen years and, I am sure, beyond.

During my recovery phase, we began to realize there was a possibility I would become a quadraplegic. This was an extremely trying time for both myself and family. A couple of things occurred to me that gave me the strength to carry on and to provide a positive outlook on what I could only describe at the time as a disaster.

The first was a copy of the Footprints poem, of which I have now found and met the author (Margie). The second was a copy of your book, which I read with the aid of an overhead glass stand whilst in hospital and later at home. After a nearly full recovery, our church promoted your visit to Melbourne, which I attended.

Both yours and Margie's work, life and support have meant so much to me and many others, who really didn't personally know you but gained the will to continue and overcome the problem placed before us through your work.

In great appreciation,

Mike
Australia

And in that day ye shall ask me nothing. Verily, verily, I say unto you, Whatsoever ye shall ask the Father in my name, he will give it to you. Hitherto have ye asked nothing in my name: ask, and ye shall receive, that your joy may be full.

St. John 16 : 23–24

Dear Margaret:

I am writing to tell you what your poem Footprints meant to my son, and now to me. It was Christmas and I didn't want to think of my son and grandson not being here. Well, they came home on Christmas Eve and I said, "We are going to the Candlelight Service at the Christian Center. Who wants to go?" My son said, "I do." This shocked me as I had been prepared to beg him to go. When we got to the Church he saw a friend. The last time he had seen this friend was in the hospital. He had not been expected to live, yet there he was! He had accepted the Lord. The music was outstanding. My son and grandson stood together clapping their hands. When the pastor gave the altar call the three walked to the front and took a candle while standing with the others. I was numb. All the time I had prayed for my son to do this, and this very time when it wasn't in my mind God had decided to answer my prayers!

When we left the church he said "Mum, I bet you never thought you'd see me do that!" My son's name was now written in the Lamb's Book of Life. At the time I didn't know how important that would be.

One evening he called and asked, "Have you read the poem Footprints?" I said, "Yes, where did you see it?" He said, "It's hanging on the wall here where I'm house-sitting. I like it." I said, "I can't remember the whole thing but I remember that in times of trouble He is carrying us." A few days later he called again and said, "Remember the poem Footprints?" I said, "Yes, did you get the one I sent you?" He said "Yes, Mum, I understand." Now I too understand how much these words have come to mean. After his sudden death in a car accident a few months later, I just wanted to die. I couldn't handle the shock and grief. When my pastor began to pray, a calmness came over me such as I'd never felt before. I knew God was in control, not me, but that He was with me and trying to carry me if I'd just let Him and lean on Him.

I awoke about 3 a.m. and started to write. I remembered my son telling me about Footprints. In his time of trouble, in his confusion, and through our prayers to God to help him, God had answered him through the poem. The words rang in my ears, "Mum, I understand." What more could I ask of God? Peace and the presence of God! It was important that I have Footprints put on my son's gravestone.

We started out to different places to see if we could have this done. At place after place we were told "No." We finally went to see the man who takes care of the cemetery. Before we got out of the car, crying, I said to

God, "If you want Footprints on his grave then you'll have to provide it because I'm too tired and I can't go on anymore." We walked into the office. I showed the man the picture of the poem and told him I wanted it on the grave, if this was possible. He said yes. It was the first gravestone of its type made, and has now been placed on my son's grave. Again, God provided.

A friend made arrangements for me to meet you and Paul in New Brunswick. I was expecting to meet a much, much older and sophisticated lady, but instead I met a very kind and gentle person about my own age. I really had to hold back the tears when I met you. You have no idea what one poem had come to mean to me. It had brought peace to my son and has brought peace to me many times since, both through receiving the poem myself and in giving it to others. How could this come about, how could I have possibly met the author of Footprints? I believe God arranged it.

Vera
Alberta

These things I have spoken unto you, that in me ye might have peace. In the world ye shall have tribulation: but be of good cheer: I have overcome the world.

St. John 16 : 33

"*L*ord, You told me when I decided to follow You,

You would walk and talk with me all the way.

But I'm aware that during the most troublesome

times of my life there is only one set of footprints.

I just don't understand why, when I needed You most,

You leave me."

Dear Mrs. Powers:

I read your book *Footprints* this evening and am inspired to write to you and tell you how very much your beautiful poem has meant to me.

In 1969 or 1970 I was about twelve or thirteen years old and did not yet know the Lord. I was, however, about to enter a crisis in my life that would last the rest of my teen years. One night back then, I really did "have a dream" whereby the Lord revealed to me that my mother was having an affair. I did not know it was the Lord at the time who revealed this to me, and all I ever remembered of the dream was a horrible sinking feeling about the knowledge and, for some strange reason, a vision of some footprints on a beach. This scene stayed with me over the years, but I could never figure out what those footprints in the sand were supposed to mean.

In the meantime, of course, I have read your poem many times and have been touched by its profound meaning. I also became a Christian in the early 1970s.

It wasn't until just last year, however, during an extremely emotional crisis, that I was praying and happened to reflect upon the dream I'd had so many years ago. Again, the image of footprints in the sand appeared for just the briefest moment. What did it mean? And at that instant God answered my question. In a flash I realized the significance of your lovely poem Footprints to my dream. It was so obvious, but why had I not realized it before?

As a young girl my Lord was warning me of a disaster to come—and that He would carry me through those difficult times ahead, just as He was carrying me at that very moment.

I cried and thanked the Lord for all the times He had carried me and then, in a simple request, I asked Him to provide me with a copy of the poem. And I thought, "Now, how is He going to do that?" The very same evening I picked up a book I had been reading, *Love Must Be Tough* by Dr. James Dobson, and after reading a few pages, there before my eyes was the copy I'd requested of Footprints.

I'm sorry you had to go through so much heartache about the poem, but it has been such a blessing to me that I feel as if the words of the poem came straight from the Lord God Himself.

Sincerely,

Lorrissa
California

Nevertheless I am continually with thee: thou hast holden me by my right hand. Thou shalt guide me with thy counsel, and afterward receive me to glory.

Psalm 73 : 23–24

Dear Margaret:

I just finished reading your little book, *Footprints*, that was published in 1993. I have for many years been encouraged by that thoughtful poem and impressed with its anonymity. It seemed fitting that such a divinely inspired message bore no name of authorship when I first read it.

I am reminded of a song written by a Christian man, that is seen often printed without any credit to him. His name is Noel Paul Stookey and the song he wrote is undoubtedly familiar to you: "The Wedding Song." I remember hearing him once explain why his name often does not appear along with the sheet music. He said that it was a song which seemed to come straight from God, and as such he wasn't interested in taking credit for it. I hope you understand me when I say that those words impressed me deeply, and carried over to my reaction to the poem I have always known as Footprints.

Even though your work was pirated and others illegally profited from it, the anonymity of the poem has, I believe, intensified the divine message behind it. In other words, good has come from what was evil—God has used your loss for His gain. Surely your reward is waiting for you in Heaven.

Having said that, I am glad to have bought your book, giving you at least some financial profit for your work as its poet. I enjoyed reading it, tears and all. God bless you in your continued ministry.

Together in Christ,

Kevin
Pennsylvania

. . . behold, I will pour out my spirit unto you, I will make known my words unto you.

Proverbs 1 : 23

Dear Margaret:

I purchased your book *Footprints*. This was the most rewarding, inspiring book I have ever read, besides the Bible. I am very happy and pleased that you published this book.

I had quite the happy moment when I read the chapter in which you and your future husband walked along the beach that inspired this poem. My husband and I gave this poem to one another as a reminder of our faith. What a confirmation!

Please let me tell you that somehow, through all these years, I remembered your poem as you originally wrote it. I never even noticed a variation in any of the poems that were copied until I read your book. I know that God did as He promised. The Holy Spirit interpreted the poem for me as God had inspired you. The same! I also remember the poem as "I Had a Dream." However, looking for the poem under the correct title, I discovered, was impossible.

Your poem has been passed to many. It has helped to keep the faith and has given hope. My children and I have lived by your poem. You have been blessed and have inspired so many.

Your poem brought me through a very bad childhood.

I have turned my past into giving and understanding to help others. The lesson I learned was that sometimes things happen and we are not to understand the reason why. Accept it, cherish it, and move on, in love. The best is, I knew God was carrying me.

Thank you for giving, for allowing God to use you and, best of all, for the poem that has inspired me for so many years. I can share with others your book *Footprints* to help give them a deeper love of God, and hope.

Love to you always,

Karen
Washington

*I will instruct thee and teach thee in the way which thou shalt go:
I will guide thee with mine eye.*

Psalm 32 : 8

Dear Margaret:

I just finished your book *Footprints* and wanted to let you know that I am one of the millions who were deeply impressed by your poem.

Last summer I went through a bizarre experience that shook me to my foundations and made me feel that I was in danger of losing my mind. Although I believe that God never gives us more than we can handle in the way of difficulties, I really believed that He may have misjudged my ability to carry on in this case. I really didn't know if I could make it through. I've always loved your poem, which I thought was anonymous, ageless and timeless, and I kept reminding myself that even though I felt as if I'd been abandoned, I was really being carried.

If your poem took me through Step One, perhaps your book will help me through Step Two. As I went through the experience, my husband stood by me all the way as did my family, even though they didn't understand what was happening. It really helped me to read about someone else who has obviously been on a spiritual path for many years, and to hear her discuss her own experience.

I'm sorry you had to go through what you did when

your poem was stolen and plagiarized, but without that event occurring the story behind your poem may not have been able to touch my life because probably your book wouldn't have been written. God really does move in mysterious ways.

With gratitude and love,

Linda
Manitoba

For he hath not despised nor abhorred the affliction of the afflicted; neither hath he hid his face from him; but when he cried unto him, he heard.

Psalm 22 : 24

I have recently read your story relating the life of the poem always known to me as Footprints. My mother found the story at our local Christian bookstore and knew how significant your words have been to me since I was a pre-teen.

I saw Footprints very soon after its unfortunate loss. As I recall, I was twelve years old and at a local arts and crafts fair. Your poem was immortalized on a wooden plaque. The words you wrote before I was born touched me in a way no words have touched me since. At twelve, my life challenges were, in many ways, still to come. But as the years passed and God inevitably taught me through challenges, Footprints was always there to remind me that God would be with me always, as long as I kept my heart open to Him.

Today, at twenty-five, I have many copies of your meaningful words. Motivational speakers advise us to have visible reminders of the things in life you want most. Footprints is in the rooms of my house that I use most often and I read it frequently.

Your misfortune in losing "I Had a Dream" became my inspiration and that of many of my friends. I am sure you have received many letters of this nature, but it seems truly an injustice that you suffered such feelings of hopelessness at the same time as I was gaining so much hope from your words. I can only hope that through letters such as mine, you will gain a sense of how much faith your initial loss has given to many people. My understanding and empathy with your words, I believe, are God's reward for your wonderful gift of poetry.

In God,

Vicki
Washington

I will delight myself in thy statutes: I will not forget thy word.
Psalm 119 : 16

Dear Margaret:

I just finished the book *Footprints: The True Story Behind The Poem That Inspired Millions*, and was deeply moved. Your poem "I Had a Dream" has held a special meaning for me and my mother for several years.

I first saw this poem in the hands of a native man in an isolated community in northern Ontario. This man had just lost his son. I had gone to visit him and there I found him holding your poem in his hands. This was in September 1983. I was a Grade Two teacher in this northern native community for three years. It was special to realize that the poem had been penned quite close to Camp Iawah, and not so very long ago.

I can relate closely to your struggle to let go of bitterness, trying to make everything right and learning to give everything to God. I empathize with you. "I Had a Dream" has brought comfort to my mother and I am sure to countless others.

One thought came to mind at Camp Iawah that I hope brings you comfort. It is this: by your poem going missing, it has become well known to millions and a tremendous source of comfort to so many. It is a real mystery. And although there has been considerable pain, there is beauty and light in your story.

The story told in *Footprints: The True Story* seems to be so interwoven with many places and experiences in my life that I was inspired to write to you. I hope you find this letter of interest.

Sincerely,

Bruce
Ontario

For as the sufferings of Christ abound in us, so our consolation also aboundeth by Christ.

II Corinthians 1 : 5

$\mathcal{H}$e whispered, "My precious child,

I love you and will never leave you,

never, ever, during your trials and testings.

When you saw only one set of footprints

it was then that I carried you."

Dear Margaret:

Footprints has had a great effect on my life. It gave me strength during one particular incident in my life that I'd like to share with you.

It was March 10, 1991, when my fiancé and I were hit by a vehicle travelling at approximately seventy miles per hour. We were hit in the passenger side, where I was sitting, and my feet were pinned beneath the wreck. Spitting parts of my teeth out while covered in blood, I was in shock. You see, it was my wedding year and I was to be married August 31, five and one-half months away. In the hospital I was stuck with needles and X-rayed from head to toe. I suffered cracked ribs and a broken shoulder bone, lost some teeth, had a broken nose, and was scarred on my nose and chin. I also had the upper tissue in my gums severed, and to this day I still don't have any feeling there. I waited so long for the day that I would happily walk down the aisle, but now it seemed that this event would not take place for at least another year.

During this time, I pulled out my bookmark with Footprints on it. I kept crying and reading, crying and reading. The hope that God was carrying me through this rough time in my life was the only thought that kept me going. I was in so much pain, both emotional and physical, that if my faith had not been there I could not have made it. Shortly after my accident my sister Mary, who suffered from mental illness, had another nervous breakdown. Would my wedding go as planned? Now I had physiotherapy, lots of dental work to be done, family stress to cope with and a wedding to plan. I brought out Footprints so many times during this period that it almost seemed as if it was part of me. I was praying to God to carry me through this time and to show me how this would make me a stronger individual.

My dental work was completed two weeks before my wedding. The aches and pains were still there, but my scars were covered with make-up. Though on medication, my sister was at the wedding, and that is what really mattered. The wedding went as planned, and I owed it all to the encouragement I got from Footprints.

My feeling is that whenever tragedy of any sort hits you, you need a way to deal with it. The best way I dealt with it was through faith in God and faith that He was with me all the way. I believed that God was carrying me through this rough time in my life, and I knew that things would work out as long as I had faith in God.

The wedding was beautiful and two months later I was expecting my daughter, who is now fifteen months old.

Footprints is indeed a magnificent piece of work that those who believe in God—and even those who don't—can use to heal their wounds and to find great strength to overcome the obstacles or tragedies that come their way. It helped me tremendously and that is why I have included it in my book, *The Key to Happiness*.

I am sure that there are many, many lives to whom this poem has given strength. I only hope that many more people will be affected by it as I have been. It will keep changing people's lives, for through it we find the courage to believe that God is watching over us and that He is guiding us and will carry us over the rough or bumpy roads.

Sincerely,

Michele
British Columbia

*He giveth power to the faint; and to them that have
no might he increaseth strength.*

Isaiah 40 : 29

Dear Margaret:

I just finished reading your book last night. I finished it in one night. I don't do something like this often, but I really felt I needed to tell you how your Footprints poem affected my life.

It was March 1983 and my life was getting on the right track. My husband and I had just gotten back together after a break-up and had had our second child. My baby brother had enlisted in the Navy the previous year and was doing well—until we got that fateful phone call. The Navy said he had been injured while aboard his ship off the coast of San Diego. We were unsure of what exactly had happened, but later found out that he had been run over by a plane during a man-overboard search. We were on our way to the naval hospital when we learned his legs had been crushed beyond repair, and that he was in surgery for a double leg amputation at that moment.

We got to the hospital and a chaplain met us. The doctor came out to prepare us for what we would see. My brother was three weeks shy of his twenty-first birthday. The chaplain asked if he could pray with us and then handed us a small business-type card. On it was the Footprints poem. I read it and thought it was ironic to receive that poem after my brother had just lost both his legs, but I clung to those words and the hope they brought.

My brother was brought back to life four times before he stabilized to stay in critical condition for several more months. He had several more amputations due to infection. When it was all over, his legs went only to the mid-thigh. The hospital had him on morphine for pain. Somehow during this time, he found out about your poem. I don't know if he heard it from me or the chaplain but he wanted everyone to know about your poem. I went to the Christian bookstore and brought him the plaque. He would show it to whoever would listen and then tell of his near-death experience.

We knew his life was spared for a reason. He even became a hero in the local town. He pulled through and has tried hard to go on with life. He overcame morphine withdrawal, life-threatening infections and so much pain, and is in a wheelchair for life. Before the accident he played drums. He took lessons for years and was very good. He wanted to play professionally, but with the accident it seemed that dream was over. But he met a man who figured out a system so that he could play again and he's as good as he ever was.

During his hospital stay (one year), my brother would

always say, "Someday I'll play my drums for Him." He still hopes to accomplish that.

After reading your book I felt so badly that you did not get the credit for it. I like to write (or must write) poems too; they are a part of me. I would feel devastated, too. But I want you to know that your poem reached me and my family just when we needed it, and though you didn't get the credit here, God gave you the glory!!

Oh—and no man had fallen overboard!

Sincerely,

Laura
California

My son, forget not my law; but let thine heart keep my commandments: For the length of days, and long life, and peace, shall they add to thee.

Proverbs 3 : 1–2

Dear Mrs Powers,

I have just finished reading your book about your authorship of the poem known as Footprints. I felt I needed to write to you to let you know what a blessing that poem has been to me, and especially how it helped me through a very trying time in my life.

On December 13, 1988, I became ill with a rare neurological illness known as Guillain Barré Syndrome (GBS), caused by my own immune system. During the onset of GBS, and during its critical stage and the plateau that occurs before healing begins, I could pray only a childlike prayer of, "Jesus, gentle shepherd, please carry your lamb." In my mind's eye, I saw a picture of Jesus as the shepherd carrying the lamb—which was me! I often thought of your poem and envisioned that one set of footprints as he carried me. What a comfort!

If one is going to have pain with GBS, as I did, it is at its worst during the plateau, which for me lasted two weeks. The pain was like being consumed by a white fireball. The hypodermics helped only partially, for I could have them only every four hours and their effectiveness never lasted that long. It was during this waiting time, while in pain, that I prayed most fervently to be carried. One afternoon as I was praying, my prayer changed. I asked God to let me know that He was carrying me. Immediately, I was conscious of being in His arms! He was carrying me in His right arm as we would an infant. He was dazzlingly white. All was quiet. I was free from pain. What peace! But I wasn't content. I wanted more! So I asked Him to let me see the one set of footprints He was making as He carried me. I *turned* my head towards His shoulder—remember, this is when I was paralyzed—and I looked and I saw only one set!

I have no idea how long I was with Jesus. I can tell you the circumstances just prior to my prayer, but nothing immediately following it. Perhaps He allowed me to sleep. I know the pain lessened thereafter.

This experience has changed me spiritually! The Lord is so very real and dear to me. Death has no fear for me; I long for the day when Heaven becomes my home!

Perhaps knowing a little of how God used your poem to help me through the darkest days of my life will help ease some of the sense of loss you felt when others took the credit for your beautiful poem. All I can say is, "God bless you!" And . . . THANK YOU!

Sincerely, in Jesus!

Joyce
Massachusetts

He restoreth my soul: he leadeth me in the paths of righteousness for his name's sake.

Psalm 23 : 3

Dear Mrs. Powers:

As a resource and methods teacher at a local junior high school for many years, I have dealt with many disturbed teenagers—perhaps none more so than a girl named Sue.

Sue was a sixteen-year-old girl who started attending my classes after having been expelled from every other junior high available to her. At that time she was living with her mother, but had endured many years of periodic visits from an alcoholic father. The mother was on social assistance and really showed little love and concern for Sue. Thus Sue lived most of the time on the streets.

I endeavored to spend as much time as I could with her and had many noon-hour and after-school talks with her. We appeared to make little progress in helping her straighten out her life and establish a purpose for living.

Much to my concern and dismay, Sue remained with us for only two months. She decided she couldn't handle any more, and one night ran away with her boyfriend. All I could do now was pray for her, having no idea where she was or under what circumstances she was living.

About a year and one-half later, I received a letter from Sue enclosing a copy of your Footprints poem. After having gone down to the depths about as far as she could go, she had started thinking about some of the things we had discussed and a copy of your poem came into her hands. After reading it several times over a twenty-four hour period, and shedding many tears, she told me she began to realize that the only way she could straighten out her life and get on the right path was to let God "carry" her. It was the Holy Spirit touching her through your pain that brought her to the point of yielding and hopefully accepting Christ. It was a broken, changed girl who wrote that letter. It was such a blessing to me; I thought it might also be to you.

In Christ,

Leta
New Brunswick

For he shall deliver the needy when he crieth; the poor also, and him that hath no helper. He shall spare the poor and needy, and shall save the souls of the needy.

Psalm 72 : 12–13

Dear Margaret:

When I first read your poem Footprints, like thousands of others who have read it, I wept. My heart responded to the truth in the words. This was several years before it became known that you were the author. I had thanked God for "Author Unknown," for the someone who was able to express in words what had been my personal experience. The years of being a young widow with two children were not easy, and there were times when I simply could not understand where God was in all of our circumstances—times when I was so overcome by grief and aloneness that I would cry out to God that I just could not continue because it was all too overwhelming. But always after a night of weeping there would come the peace that only the Father could give and the assurance that He had promised. He would be a husband to me and a Father to my children. He asked me only to trust Him.

Two songs come to mind that have had a special meaning for me: "Through it All," by André Crouch, and a song by Scott Wesley Brown called "He Will Carry You." Then came the poem Footprints, which again was a reminder and an affirmation of all the times God has been so faithful, even though at times I was not always aware of this perfect faithfulness and love. I want you to know what a blessing your poem and the story of your life has been to me.

God's blessings,

Lorraine
British Columbia

My flesh and my heart faileth: but God is the strength of my heart, and my portion for ever.

Psalm 73 : 26

Dear Mrs. Powers:

I am writing to you this beautiful morning to thank you for your encouraging poem, Footprints. It must surely be inspired by God. I have over the years enjoyed the gentle words. A few years ago I had cause to reflect upon them more thoughtfully. They had new meaning for me because of the circumstances in which I found myself. My family and I found ourselves in the wrong place at the wrong time back in 1990, for we were in Kuwait when Iraq invaded and so got caught up—along with many others—as hostages. For me this was a very frightening time. My husband was taken at gunpoint on the second day, and I along with my two children and other women and children fended for ourselves. It's a long story but thank God all ended well.

Two years after our ordeal was over, and by now having grown in my Christian faith and put my life fully into the hands of our Lord, life held one more nightmare in store for me. In October 1992, my husband and I had a believers' baptism. I had been a church attender for most of my life, but now things were different. I really wanted God to play an important part in my life as my personal LORD and SAVIOUR. You could say I was feeling really good and contented in my life. Little did I know that I was in for a real test of my faith.

By the end of October, and from completely out of the blue, I found myself in a mental hospital suffering from Post Traumatic Stress Disorder. I was very ill indeed. With voices in my head plaguing me night and day, I was so unstable that I needed constant surveillance. This was my rock bottom. I can't put into words just how defeated I felt, having only weeks before really committed myself to being a Christian. You can imagine my confusion. I tried hard to fight these voices and to get myself back together, but to no avail. Over the years I had tried to read the Bible, but with little success. Now, my vision was impaired and my concentration non-existent, so trying to read the Bible was a no-go. It was at this time I came to realize I could do nothing for myself. So I prayed constantly, but even this wasn't enough because the voices would answer me. Then I learned a very valuable lesson: I gave up trying to do it all myself. I took my hands off the steering wheel of my life and instead of being a self-dependent person, I became a God-dependent person. This wasn't easy for me. I had been strong through the Gulf War for my family's sake and had gotten used to the idea of being strong, but now I had to admit to myself that I was weak and helpless. It's very true that in my greatest weakness I found my greatest strength in the Lord Jesus.

As I said earlier, I knew very little of God's words spoken in the Bible except for the most commonly used scripture that was taught in the Church of England. One verse came to mind which I could use to help me: "BE STILL AND KNOW THAT I AM GOD." It may be a very small verse, but it said it all. Slowly, slowly I became well again and could return to my family. My husband was very relieved. At one point he had thought he had lost me forever.

A strange thing: when I returned home from the hospital and instantly went to look up the verse, I found it wasn't in our Good News Bible. I must say, this con-fused me. I thought I must have made it up! It was a few months later when I was looking through someone else's New International Bible that I found this verse in Psalm 46 : 10. I now read the Bible every day. Last year, for the first time, I got my very own Bible in which I can underline and write in the margin. I love my New International Bible; it means so much to me.

Your poem Footprints is very special because it puts into words just how I feel, that God really did carry me in my deepest despair and helplessness until I was strong enough to walk. When, and only when, I was strong enough to walk did he ever so gently put me down on my feet once more, then held my hand until I could walk without falling. How wonderful to think of the Lord's promises and to know that THROUGH ALL AND IN ALL circumstances we will never be alone. As for those footprints . . . yes, they will always be there. Jesus will walk with us whatever the path we take, and when we don't see the outline of His prints, with faith we know that this is the time we are being carried.

I sometimes use your poem to try and explain how close I feel to our Lord and how very much He loves each and every one of us. I wouldn't have chosen my trials, but because of them my faith has grown so much stronger that I don't regret them, either.

Love in Christ, God bless and keep you,

Sheila
England

God is our refuge and strength, a very present help in trouble.
Therefore will not we fear, though the earth be removed . . .
Psalm 46 : 1–2

Dear Margaret:

It's been such a long time since we have been in touch, but you have been in my thoughts recently and I was determined to write to you. One of the reasons that I have been thinking of you is the poem, Footprints which I have discovered you wrote in 1964. I found an article about it at the Christian bookstore and also someone had brought it to my attention not too long ago. They knew that it was very special to me.

A friend showed it to me nine years ago after my husband had a terrible accident and we didn't know if he would survive. At the time the Lord gave me such peace that people were amazed because they knew how I could panic. When I read Footprints, I looked at my friend and said, "That's what happened to me. He carried me." And He has carried me so many times since then. My husband recovered, Praise God!

I am so thrilled to think a dear friend of mine wrote that. Oh, how it has been used to encourage those who are going through hard times! We have been through some pretty awful things in the past few years, and it has not been easy, but God is faithful and He has been holding us all along the way. Through all of this we are learning to know Him in a very special way.

I thank God that because Jesus came we have a hope that nothing can take away, and His peace is so precious. Take care and God bless and keep you in His tender care.

Much love,

Cathie
Quebec

And the peace of God, which passeth all understanding, shall keep your hearts and minds through Christ Jesus.
Philippians 4 : 7

Dear Mrs. Powers:

I recently read your book, *Footprints*. I was very touched by your story, and was reduced to tears several times.

Two weeks ago, my mother-in-law gave me a copy of your book, which she had read some time ago, a thank-you note I had written in November 1993 to be published in our children's school newsletter—and a copy of your poem. I thoroughly enjoyed reading the story behind the poem. It has great meaning to me, for God truly has picked me up and carried me through the most difficult times in my life. The worst was in October 1993.

On Saturday, October 2, 1993, my husband, forty-one years old, came home from golfing with a severe headache. He would not eat or drink anything for days and complained that his eyeballs hurt and that he could not sleep. He was given antibiotics and pain medication which would help him sleep. He continued to get worse in spite of the fact that he told me he was getting better. On Saturday I became alarmed because he had trouble talking. I called a good friend and asked him to come over and observe my husband. After visiting for an hour or so, he suggested I give him lots of liquids and make him eat something. Sunday, when the children and I returned home from church, I was again concerned. His parents stopped by to see how he was feeling, and were puzzled when I mentioned to them, "I am so glad you are here." They commented that his color was better and that perhaps we should wait another forty-eight hours.

Shortly after his parents left, my husband tried to say something, but I couldn't understand him. I gave him a pencil and a pad of paper and asked him to write down what he was trying to say. He wrote the words, "we came are." I then knew I had to get him to the hospital.

The hospital is approximately five miles from our home but by the time we arrived he could hardly speak. He was not able to say what year it was, who was currently the President of the United States, or even his own name. His right side became paralysed. On Monday an MRI revealed that he had a large aneurysm on the left side of the brain. I was told he would have to have a craniotomy. I felt very lost, afraid and alone on the fifth floor Intensive Care Unit of the hospital. I also felt a strong urging to go to my church. I went, and met one of our associate ministers (a good friend). Together we prayed and asked for God's abiding love and grace to sustain us. I was left at home alone. I can't recall if it was that night or early the next morning when "I placed my burden at His feet." I got down on my knees and prayed. I surrendered my heart to God, telling him that this situation was totally out of my control. There was nothing I could do to make things better. I needed Him to throw His arms around me and give me strength. I asked Him to comfort my husband and help guide and direct us. My prayer was answered and God gave me an abundant amount of strength. I had to be strong for my husband and our three children and his family as well.

The neurosurgeon told me matter-of-factly that we had two choices. We could either wait eleven days for the swelling to go down and the blood vessels to quit going into spasms before performing surgery, or, he could perform the surgery now. Although he preferred to wait, he also expressed the urgency of the situation by saying, "It makes my heart hurt to see a man my own age lying there as sick as your husband. I can't promise you that if we take him into surgery now that he will make it off the operating table." His condition was failing rapidly and I could see that time was of the essence.

I asked his parents (who live locally) to be at the hospital when the doctors talked with me to help with the decision that had to be made. His father made the comment that, "My son is a fighter and he would want us to go ahead." We all agreed and shortly thereafter he was prepped for surgery. I remember his father asking me if the neurosurgeon was a Christian. I did not know but later discovered he was. Now I had the difficult task of telling our three small children (ages twelve, ten, and seven) that their daddy did not have the flu but was having brain surgery. I was honest with them and told them that their daddy may not make it through this. We all prayed together and then I left to go back to the hospital.

It was heartwarming to see the number of friends and family members in the ICU waiting room that night. There must have been ten or twenty people there. My mom and dad arrived after driving twelve hours to get there. We all gathered in a circle and prayed. Prayers went up from everywhere. Concerned friends called the local Christian radio stations and various prayer groups. Three couples from our Sunday School class who had heard the news came to comfort me. One of the couples actually worked in the out-patient surgery during the day and came back that night to keep us informed.

After my husband had been in surgery for some time, we were told that as soon as the area had been prepared and opened, the aneurysm had burst. His main artery had to be shut down for three minutes, but in spite of that, everything had gone as well as could be expected. In fact, around midnight, when they brought him back to ICU from the recovery room, he gave a "thumbs up" signal to me. This was a good sign. But he was not out of danger and would be in critical condition for the next seventy-eight hours.

The next day the surgeons told me that he would not be able to speak due to the brain damage he had sustained. I was just thankful that he was alive. He was diagnosed as being apraxic and aphasic. All he could say after the operation was the word "no." He recognized us, but did not remember our names. Sixteen months have passed and he is still attending speech therapy, but now only twice a week. He has come a long way even though the process has been, in his words, "slow."

We are very grateful for the outpouring of expressions of love we received through calls, cards, flowers, prayers, meals, visits, and more. Now you can understand why I so very much enjoyed reading your book *Footprints*. Praise be to God from whom all blessings flow.

Donna
Florida

Blessed be the Lord, that hath given rest unto his people Israel, according to all that he promised: there hath not failed one word of all his good promise . . .

I Kings 8 : 56

Dear Ms. Powers:

Recently I received your book *Footprints: The True Story Behind The Poem That Inspired Millions* for Christmas. I was moved and inspired. I must first tell you that I have many copies of this poem, including one that I carry with me at all times in my wallet. The first time I read this poem a chill went through me and tears came to my eyes. I also felt a chill when I read some of your stories, especially the ones about your daughter's angels. The thought of everybody having an angel to watch over them fascinates me. I can only hope that "my angel" is as good to me as your daughter's angel is to her. You definitely taught me a lesson about not being bitter, and how to let God play a large role in my life. I am at a time now when I need God to guide and "carry" me. I only hope that what your poem describes will come true for me.

Sincerely,

Rebecca
Pennsylvania

Behold, I send an Angel before thee, to keep thee in the way, and to bring thee into the place which I have prepared.

Exodus 23 : 20

Dear Margaret:

I am writing to let you know how your poem Footprints has touched my life. I had read your poem and thought it was nice, but it had no personal meaning to me at that time. However, this all changed during our trip to England and Scotland in the fall of 1989.

We were driving on a two-lane highway approaching the town of Pitlochry in Scotland. I was studying the map and when I looked up, to my horror, we were on the right-hand side of the road and a car was approaching us at top speed. I knew we were going to have a head-on collision. Without thinking, I grabbed the wheel, steered off the road and drove down an embankment into the ditch. When the car finally came to a stop my husband, partly in shock, was yelling. I kept saying, "We're alive, we're alive!" We ended up hugging each other with tears in our eyes. I felt such a joy that we had been spared from what, I am sure, would have been a tragic accident. Oddly enough we were not injured in any way and our car, which we thought would be damaged, didn't even have a scratch on it. We were able to bring the car back up a lengthy distance and drive out of the ditch without having a tow truck. We were shaken up but thankful to God for being alive.

Your poem came back to me at that time. I wasn't satisfied until I obtained a copy of it to read once again. At once your words had meaning to me and touched my heart. I have always felt God's presence in my life, but on that road in Scotland I believe that God intervened in our lives and picked up our car and carried it to safety.

I thank God for His loving care, and I thank you for expressing His will so meaningfully.

With sincere gratitude,

Evelyn
Ontario

But whoso hearkeneth unto me shall dwell safely, and shall be quiet from fear of evil.

Proverbs 1 : 33

Dear Margaret:

For many years I have loved and appreciated your poem Footprints. It has had a profound influence on my life. My love for God is very deep, and your poem has sent a beautiful message to me whenever pain and hurt have clouded my path and I felt like I was walking alone in this journey through life.

In this letter, I would like to share with you some of the very difficult trials and testings I have experienced in my life. It is very emotional to write about these painful experiences, but I pray that I will write this with openness and clarity and fully express that all glory goes to God for my healing. He is the divine healer. God has blessed you, Margaret, with the beautiful gift of writing. I hope that this letter will express to you the many blessings you have given to my family and myself.

My father was killed in a very tragic plane crash when I was six and it became impossible for me as a child to understand that God truly loved me and would protect me. For years I questioned, "How could He be a loving God to take my Daddy like that?" My life was filled with so many unanswered questions and buried pain. By the time I reached adulthood, my life was ruled by many fears. Within my fragile shell, there was a tremendous fear of death. As I looked out into the busy world, I did not find answers, only more pain and tragedy being reported daily in the media.

When I became a new mom, I felt overwhelmed with responsibility for this new life. At this time a very special Christian woman came into my life and gently shared God's love with me. Through her sincere expression of God's love, I came to know Jesus Christ. My heart was renewed and it felt like life had a real purpose. God became my Father and although there was still a sting in my heart from my Dad's tragic death, God removed all the fear and anxiety surrounding it. A few months later, my husband Ray came to know the Lord at a presentation of the Jesus film. We were baptized a few weeks later and it was the beginning of a new life together, walking with Jesus.

My first experience with Footprints was as a gift in celebration of our baptism from the friend who had led me to the Lord. I was deeply touched at how the poem so beautifully illustrated how He will always be there, in good times and bad. We placed it on our wall, but it has forever been etched in our hearts.

Life is forever changing, and the years seemed to pass by so quickly. Ray and I appeared to be growing spiritually, but it seemed so slow in comparison to how very fast-paced our lives were becoming. With five children in tow, we seemed to be chasing life. It seemed so very much easier to flip on the TV than to pick up the Bible. We were entering a desert, and I found myself longing for the intimacy with God that I had had in the earlier days. I found myself questioning this busy life and all its twisted values. Still, I knew in my heart that God was sovereign and that He knew the plan for my life. Learning to put all my trust in Him was about to become my life's greatest challenge.

A visit to my doctor and a pregnancy test revealed that another whole new life had begun within me. I felt renewed and there was a well of joy within my soul. I could focus on that little life and I felt it lift me out of my sadness. I surprised my husband with the news at the beach. Our baby was his birthday present, and his birthday card read, "HAPPY BIRTHDAY, HONEY, OUR BABY IS DUE IN MAY." He was so surprised and overjoyed that he jumped up from the park bench and yelled, "We are going to have a baby!" We shared this good news with our children and together we celebrated and looked forward to the exciting months ahead.

In January, Ray and I experienced the most painful and tragic loss of our lives. Through a routine ultrasound on January 19, our baby was tragically diagnosed with anencephaly, a fatal neural tube defect. My heart filled with deep sorrow as the doctor watched the screen and told us they could not get a good image of our baby's head. Sorrow, disbelief and shock filled my soul. The ultrasound specialist and technician were not able to discuss our baby's condition with us, and all we knew was that something was terribly wrong. Immediately we were sent over to our family physician.

Our doctor's office is situated across the street from the hospital, and I will never forget that walk. I felt like collapsing. It took every ounce of my strength to walk into the office. We were comforted by our doctor, who is a Christian, but it brought on unbearable pain to hear him say, "Your baby is incompatible with life and cannot survive outside the womb." At first, our doctor felt it was probably best to end the pregnancy through early induction of labor so that we could, hopefully, move on with our lives. Early labor at twenty-one weeks would have immediately ended our baby's life. We respected our doctor's medical opinion but we could not envision terminating the little life within me.

We tried to compose ourselves for the difficult drive to pick up our children after school, but we knew we could not keep it from them. Sorrow was written all over our faces. At home, we sat together, and the tears just kept flowing all through the evening. We called our church prayer chain and asked for prayer. Before our children's bedtime, we all gathered together in prayer. It felt like a dark curtain had fallen upon us. We asked God to help us and we gave our little baby back to Him in prayer. As we shared our tears that night, God brought us all a healing night's rest.

In the morning, I felt a deep peace within my spirit ("And the peace of God, which passeth all understanding, shall keep your hearts and minds through Christ Jesus." Philippians 4 : 7) and felt the dark curtain gradually lifting. Our baby was still moving about which brought comfort to me. Later that day, we went to Grace Hospital for more testing, but the diagnosis was confirmed. Words cannot express the sorrow Ray and I felt as we watched our baby move about on the screen. The ultrasound was very detailed and the doctors shared with us that we were having a little girl. She was so carefree and comfortable, and her little hands moved about in search of her mouth. She was perfect everywhere except for her brain development. It seemed so unfair and cruel, and our hearts asked God, "Why?" I didn't feel bitter, but I did ask God, "I don't want riches and fancy things—why can't I have another little life to love?"

Our doctors were very sensitive to our pain but they

had to discuss the difficult options we had. Our first option was a "D & C," which is an abrupt termination of pregnancy, also known as an abortion. Our second option was to have an induction of labor at this early stage, give birth and hopefully get on with our lives. Our third and last option was to carry our baby to term. It was explained to us that anencephalic babies are rarely brought to term, most are aborted, either naturally or through medical intervention.

We left the hospital with a feeling of numbness and fatigue. Perhaps that was God's way of protecting us from our pain. Later that evening, we gathered together in prayer and again committed our baby to the Lord. We named her Christiana Shere and she became such a part of our family on that special night. We knew in our hearts that we could not end our baby's life, but at times we were overwhelmed knowing that she faced such severe complications. Ray and I openly shared our fears and thoughts with each other and it sometimes crossed our minds that perhaps the merciful thing to do was to start the early labor and give birth. But how can you put a date to your child's death, plan it and say it was *merciful*?

A community of believers pulled together. We were truly upheld by prayer. Three days after the diagnosis I found, through prayer, the will of the Lord. A friend called me and prayed with me over the phone. Her prayer, "Just as God protected Shere in her mother's womb, so shall He protect this child and *He* will fulfill the number of her days." That prayer profoundly touched my spirit and clearly spoke to me that God was in control of our child's life. My friend read Exodus 23 : 25–26 and from that moment on, I felt God sending me a message that He would fulfill the number of her days.

We informed the specialists of our desire to carry our baby to term. They acknowledged that our decision was rare. A few people questioned our decision and asked, "Do you fully understand what you are doing?" We stood firm in our conviction in the sanctity of life. God truly blessed us and brought beauty through our tragedy. He lifted our spirits and filled us with a peace that the world could not explain.

The beautiful poem Footprints had always inspired me. At this time in my life, I could truly feel the beauty of its message. I knew that the days ahead were going to be very difficult, but I felt comforted knowing that God would carry Christiana and I through this painful journey. For my husband Ray, at times the pain was almost unbearable as he watched and felt our baby playfully move within me. Her life seemed so carefree and healthy, it was very hard for both Ray and me to fully comprehend what her diagnosis meant.

In the days ahead, God renewed my joy for the little life within me. Each day became very special. I realized that if this was all the life I could give her and all the love I could share, then I was determined to infuse every ounce of love into her during those precious few months. It was not a sacrifice, it was the loving thing to do. She was my precious child.

Time seemed to pass so quickly, and I felt so many times that I just wanted time to stand still. I wanted to carry her within me forever. The doctors had informed us that Christiana could die at any time, but most often babies afflicted with anencephaly die during labor or shortly after birth. We were so thankful to God for each new day we had with our little Christiana. She brought joy to our children as they felt her playful kicks and reassuring movements. It was so beautiful to watch our children surround this precious life within me with love. She was treated to endless music, her brothers and sisters' piano and violin, and my flute playing. I loved to play my flute to her and I could feel her respond as I played.

The days drew closer to the end of my pregnancy and I did not want to let go of our little Christiana. I wanted to carry her forever, but I realized that God loved her and He would take good care of her. (It is very emotional to share about her because it was so very tragic and yet beautiful at the same time.) We chose not to have her heartbeat monitored during labor, as we had peace that her life rested in His hands. We were filled with a heaven-sent joy when the doctors told us she survived labor, but they said she didn't have much time. They passed her to me quickly because she was having some difficulty breathing. As she entered my arms and I spoke gently and prayed with her, she miraculously calmed and her breathing improved. I did not feel any fear and all of my energy was focused on loving her. I marvelled at her precious little face and beautiful hands. She was chubby and our family doctor spoke out and said, "A job well done, Shere!" There was such a feeling of thanksgiving in the room for each new breath she took. She was determined to live long enough to be hugged and cherished by Mom and Dad, all her brothers and sisters, close family, medical staff and her very special dedication service held in the labor/delivery room. Shortly after everyone left, Ray and I had some very intimate moments with Christiana. Her eyes were swollen from the birth, but just before she slipped away, she miraculously lifted her eyelids. I remember our special nurse, Charlene, saying,

"Look at those blue eyes." Ray and I both felt she wanted to look at Mom and Dad before she said her goodbye. As dawn approached, she peacefully slipped from her father's arms into her Heavenly Father's presence. A tape of my flute music played gently in the background as Christiana went home to Heaven.

In Christiana's short but very important life, she touched more hearts than many people touch in all their years of living. We were deeply moved by the enormous outpouring of love and support for our family. We will never forget the warmth we felt as countless prayers blanketed us with His love and peace.

Christiana sent a powerful message to the medical community that life is very precious. She was not perfect, but life is not perfect either and therefore no one had the right to take her life before His time. God is the giver of all life and life is to be valued as a most precious gift. I feel this so very deeply and, being adopted, I feel it has intensified my conviction for life. Through much pain, my birth mother unselfishly gave me life. Adoption meant that my parents could receive a gift of life. I thank God that I am alive today, and I thank Him also for the loving parents He gave me. With our baby's tragic diagnosis, I felt God was allowing me to experience the ultimate test of unconditional love. But when

I finally, "Let go and let God," the many blessings flowed and God's grace carried me.

This letter is so much longer than I intended and I hope that you can understand how important it's been for me to write and work through my thoughts and feelings. It's the first time since her death that I have relived all those months, and it's taken me some time to write this letter. I have felt a tremendous healing in sharing this with you, and I pray that God will use this for His glory.

Footprints is woven into the tapestry of my life, Margaret, and I find it so beautiful for you to become my friend when for so long you were "Author Unknown."

Love, your friend,

Shere
British Columbia

But Jesus said, Suffer little children, and forbid them not, to come unto me: for of such is the kingdom of heaven.
St. Matthew 19 : 14

Many lives have been touched by Footprints, and by the experiences and wisdom of its author, Margaret Fishback Powers. If you would like to share your story with Margaret, or respond to the thoughts expressed by the many authors of this book, you are invited to write.

Send your letters care of the publisher:

Margaret Fishback Powers
"Friends of Footprints"
c/o HarperCollins Publishers Ltd.
55 Avenue Road, Suite 2900
Toronto, Ontario, Canada
M5R 3L2